2-

Climbing Tales of Terror

Climbing Tales of Terror

by Tami Knight

Menasha Ridge Press
Birmingham, Alabama

Library of Congress Cataloging-in-Publication Data

Knight, Tami, 1959—
    Climbing tales of terror/Tami Knight. —1st ed.
        p.   cm.
    ISBN 0-89732-102-2
    1. Rock climbing—Caricatures and cartoons. 2. Snow and ice
climbing—Caricatures and cartoons. 3. Mountaineering—Caricatures
and cartoons. I. Title: Climbing tales of terror.
PN6727.K64L5 1990
741.5"973—dc20   90-46713
                                                         CIP
                                                         Rev.

Of course, this book is dedicated to The Husband & The Critter.

"NO PIG AROUND HERE !! "

HEY! BEFORE YA CONTINUE! . . . .

THE AUTHOR OF THIS TRAVESTY.

This book is a result of Mike Jones (who hopefully still works for Menasha Ridge Press) having seen one of my cartoons published in Climbing magazine. Thanks be to Lance.

As Mike soon found out, the damaged brain that had produced that vulgar, little work had indeed produced others. Specifically two comic books: LIES & SLANDER FROM A DEMENTED LITTLE CORNER OF THE COAST RANGE (Sept. 1988) and VICIOUS LIES & HEINOUS SLANDER, VOL. 2 FROM A SUPREMELY DEMENTED LITTLE CORNER OF THE COAST RANGE. (Sept. 1989)

I published 300 copies of the first which have now all found their way to variously the bottoms of bird cages, fish and chip shops, and land-fill sites. Of the 750 copies of vol. 2, hopefully they now reside in homes where the attention spans are short and the dumping times long.

"So what." you say "who cares?"

heh - heh - heh - heh - heh - heh - heh - heh - heh - heh - heh - heh - heh - heh

You might.

You may own those comics. And now you're parked on the potty ready to pinch and thinking that as you do so you'll peruse Mrs. Knight's new offering. You are suddenly enveloped by a cloying sense of deja-voo. Your dump has been coarsly interrupted by realization of betrayal .....

YOU HAVE ALREADY SEEN SOME OF THESE CARTOONS!! HORRORS! ABOM-
-INATION! DEATH!

Reeeee lacks!! Think me!!!/loooow!!! I redrew some of my faves from those books because I wanted them to reach a wider audience. It's not a heinous rip-off, it's a small rip-off for not many people. So I told you, okay???

But for most of you, virginal and pure, this will all be a New Exper-ience. So if it ISN'T time to go climbin', put away the rubber restraints and whip cream. Put up yer feet and get out the single-malt-12-year old-Och-Aye-Laddie (!) and read this cartoon book. Maybe yool laff. Perhaps yool drool. Hopefully yool do both. Hrk Hrk Hrk Hrk.

Tami Knight
Vancouver, Canada

HAIRY, LARGE & Billowing THANX to:

Mike Jones & Bob Sehlinger (I love that ay-uck-sent!) at Menasha Ridge Press, Lance Leslie at Climbing Magazine, David Harris fer his work on the comic books, Ed Spat for "proofreading" and chocolate, Megan Routley for "proof-reading" and cosmic massages, Jacq B. fer among other things, introducing us to "THE SINGLETON". "Hey Michelle, where's the store??"

HEY EX-BOYFRIEND! How do ya do!?

Stuart Wozny! Are those your real teeth?

Dear.... they are cute little mice you draw...

MOM & DAD

But do they always have to be so vulgar??

Hey!

Bini! Control your wife!

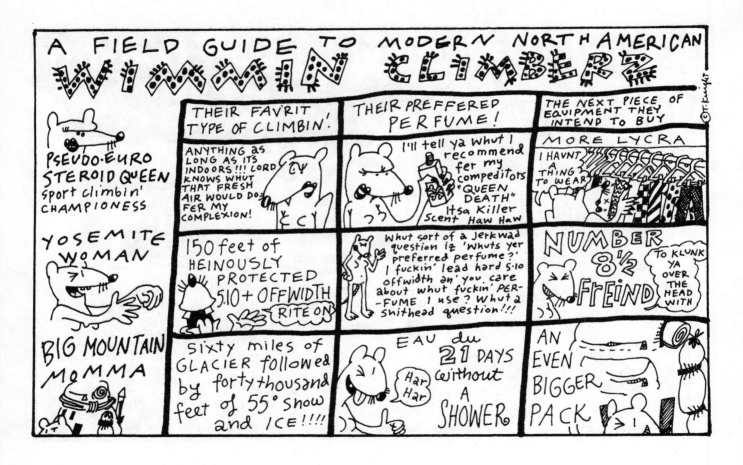

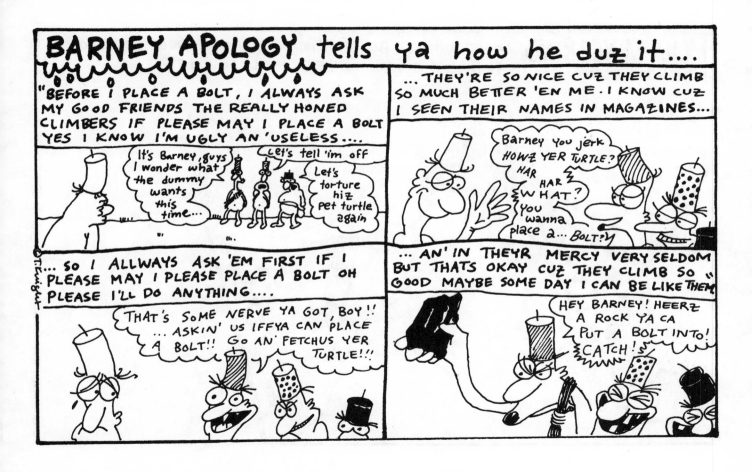

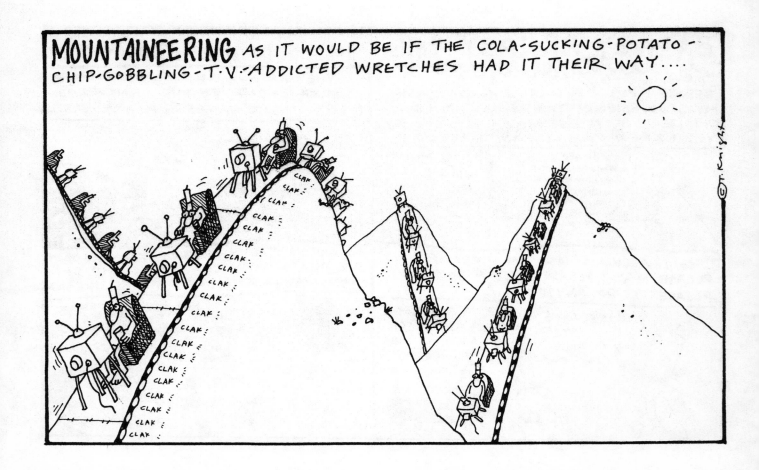

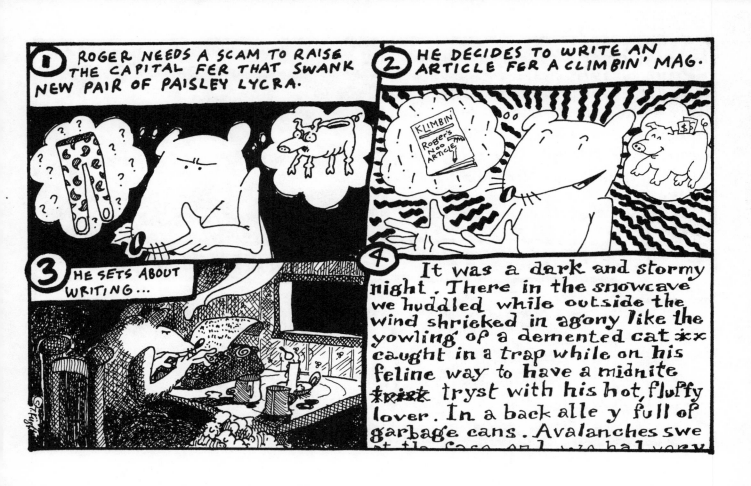

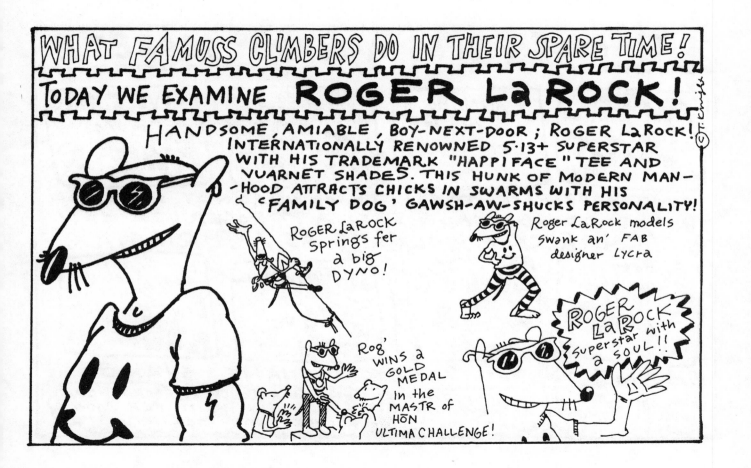

BUT!! ROGER HIDES A SORDID SECRET!!

THE FOLLOWING FILM IS RATED **XXX** ROOD & NAUGHTY

RAUNCH PICTURES presents

 BIG DADDY SAUSAGE SALIVA in 12"

 LOVE SLAVES FROM PLANET Q

THAT 'HAPPIFACE' TEE! THOSE VUARNET SHADES!! BIG DADDY SAUSAGE SALIVA?? ROGER LaROCK!! ROGER LaROCK MOONLIGHTS AS A PORN STAR??

 SIZZLIN'

 LUSHUSS

 BOW WOW WOW Ruff Ruff Woof Woof

BIG DADDY SAUSAGE SALIVA!! LOVE SLAVES from PLANET Q

SHAME ON YOU ROGER!! SHAME! SHAME!

BUT! BUT! I NEEDED MONEY! HOW ELSE COULD I AFFORD NEW LYCRA AN' NEW VUARNETS WHILE STILL PAYIN' FER MOM'S FACELIFT AN' TUMMY TUCK!! MY POOR MOM!!

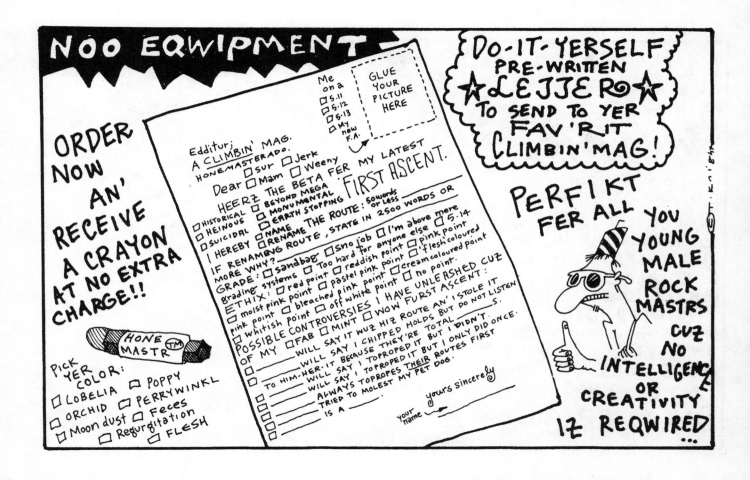

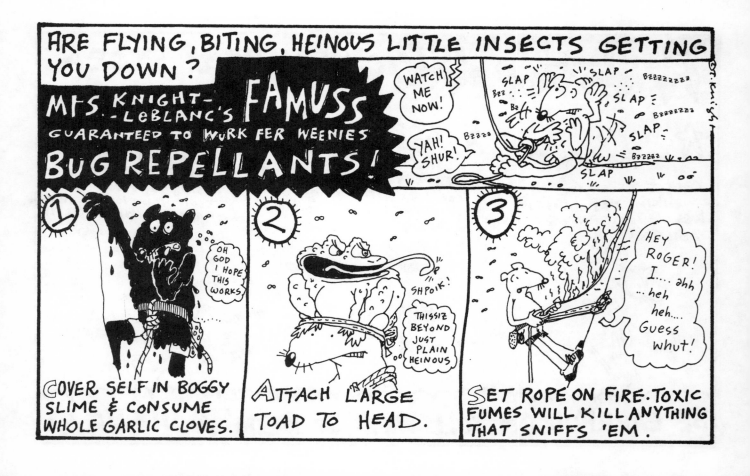

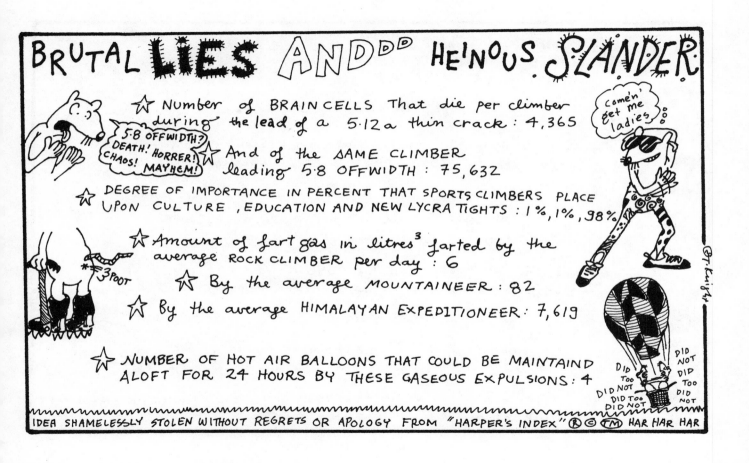

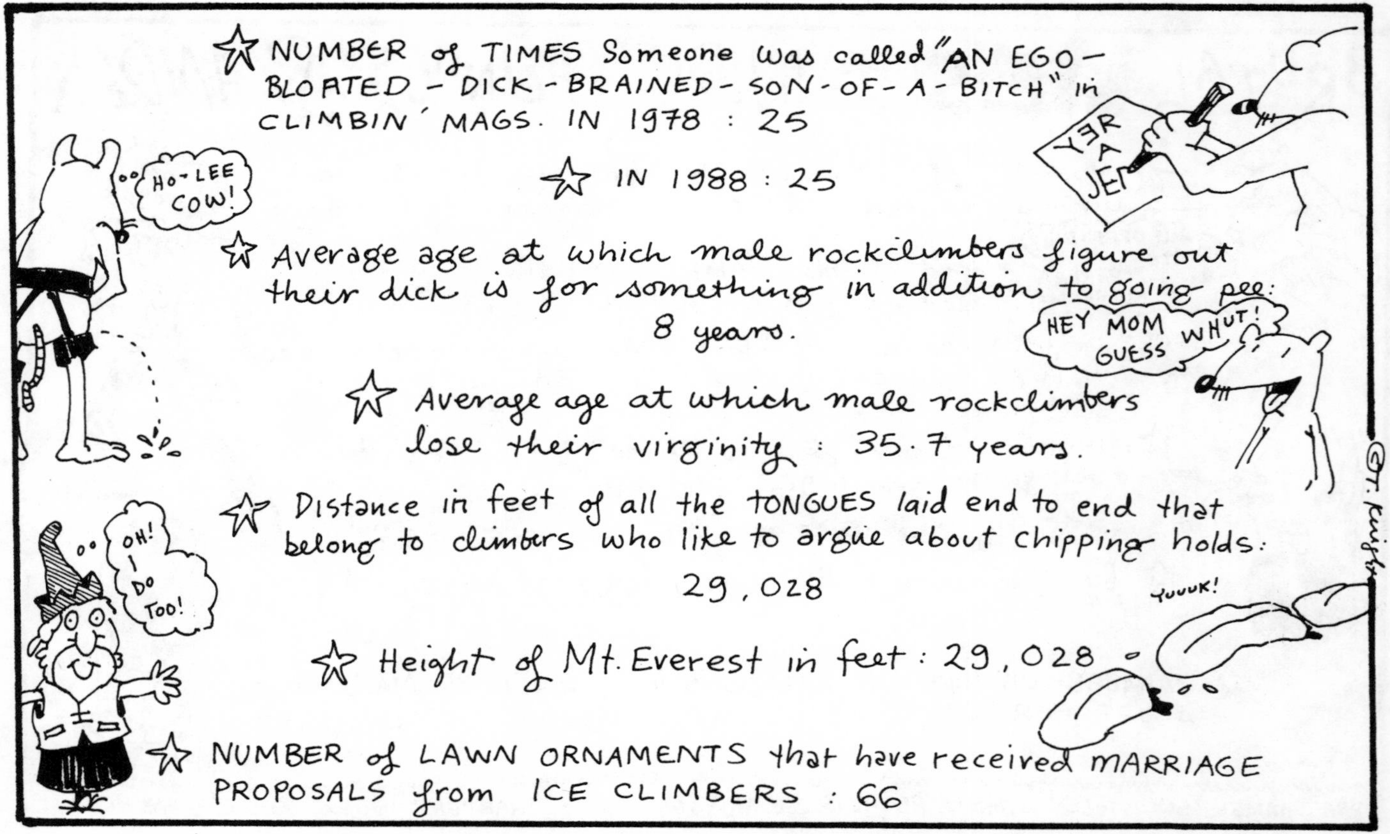
★ NUMBER of TIMES Someone was called "AN EGO-BLOATED-DICK-BRAINED-SON-OF-A-BITCH" in CLIMBIN' MAGS. IN 1978 : 25
★ IN 1988 : 25
★ Average age at which male rockclimbers figure out their dick is for something in addition to going pee: 8 years.
★ Average age at which male rockclimbers lose their virginity : 35.7 years.
★ Distance in feet of all the TONGUES laid end to end that belong to climbers who like to argue about chipping holds: 29,028
★ Height of Mt. Everest in feet : 29,028
★ NUMBER of LAWN ORNAMENTS that have received MARRIAGE PROPOSALS from ICE CLIMBERS : 66
HO-LEE COW!
YER A JE
HEY MOM GUESS WHUT!
OH! I DO TOO!
YUUUK!

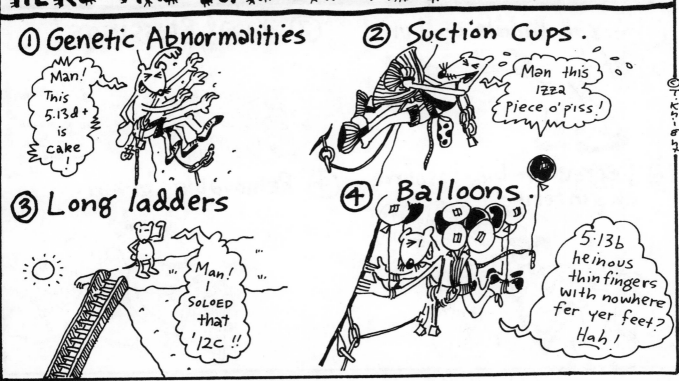

HERE ARN'T SOME EXAMPLES OF AID....

① Kayak Paddle up bum!

② Papal Blessings!

③ Degree in bio-resource engineering!

④ Removable brain.

SNO' CAVIN' MADE *AGONIZINGLY* SIMPLE!

KILLER BETA ON HOW TO DIG THE Puuurrfect SNO'CAVE!

① DRINK ½ YER WHISKY.
EAT ½ YER CHOCKLIT.

② DIG THE CAVE.

③ FINISH OFF WHISKY.
FINISH OFF CHOCKLIT.

④ PASS OUT Preferably INSIDE cave!!

SNO' CAVIN' MADE RIDICULOUSLY SIMPLE!

THINGS YA NEED TO BUILD THE PUUUURFECT SNO'CAVE!

① 12 year old, single malt whiskey.

② warm cuddly member of opposite sex.

YOUR CHOICE

③ very small and damaged brain.

④ OPTIONAL : SNOW & A BROAD-BLADE SHOVEL!!

BIG BUDDY

Glen Sno Cave

© T. Knight

SNO'CAVIN' MADE HEINOUSLY SIMPLE!!

THINGS YA DON'T NEED TO BUILD THE Puurrfect SNO'CAVE

① HUNGRY POLAR BEAR STALKING YOU.

② DEGREE IN CIVIL ENGINEERING!

③ Hypothermic partner of same sex.

④ CASE OF BEER that is SWIFTLY FREEZING!!

⑤ BALLET shoes & A TUTU!!

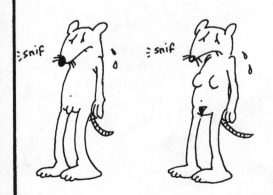

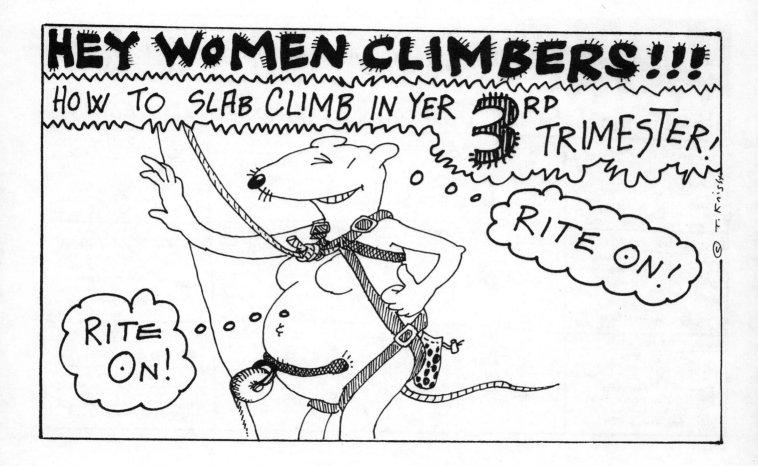

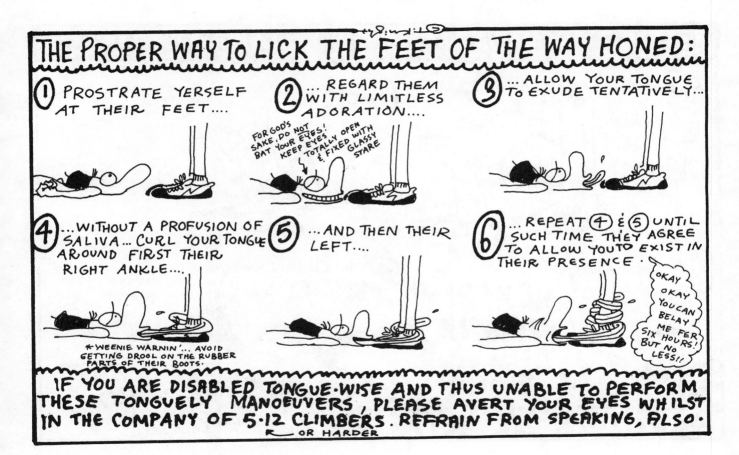

HLON.... THE COMPETITION FOR THE WRETCHED !!!

③ CHIP 'n' GOUGE

Event three involves each contestant armed with cold chisel and hammer. They must in an allotted time make the easiest possible route out of a blank wall.

④ CLIMBING SHOP RIPOFF

Next, contestants vie to remove the most amount of gear from local climbing shops without paying for it.

⑤ VICIOUS SLANDER.

Last, contestants are judged for directing pure bile towards a fellow climber. Points for odiousness, spite and vehemence.

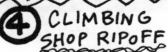

F'WANK FWANG

CLIMBING

HEY!

CANT DOG YER WAY UPPA 5.3 YOU SPOOGE FROM SPOOGEVILLE MY MUTHER CLIMBS HARD... THEN YOU & ...T NO LEGS SHF... CHICKEN YOU ...SSHOLE YA A... FOOL JERK CRETIN SHEEP CREEP WANKER

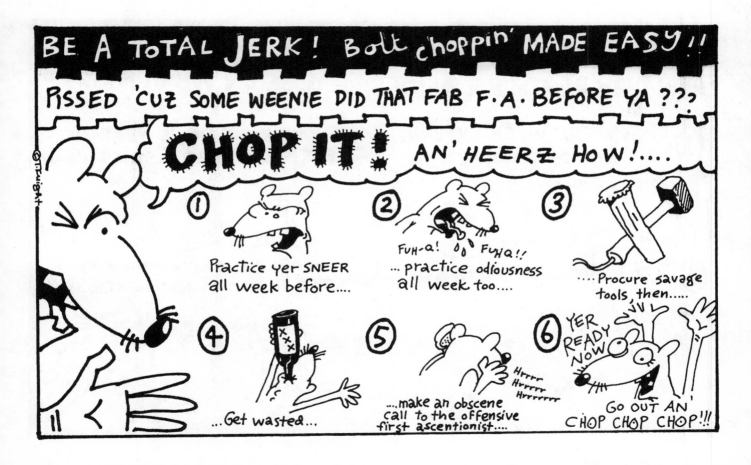

CUTE LITTLE TRIX OF THE WAY HONED...

HOW THEY REMEMBER WHICH SHOE GOES ON WHAT FOOT??

① SPEND THE WEEK PREVIOUS IN TOTAL SECLUSION....

② ... WHEN TIME IS NEAR, EYEBALL FEET & SHOES. CHANT.

③ WORK INTO A FRENZY...

④ ... COPIOUS SALIVATION WILL LEAD TO DIVINE REVELATION!!!

BUT NO! IT'S A PUERILE VICIOUS SAVAGE LIE!!!
THE TOP-QUALITY SNEER OF HŌN MASTRS ™ ® IS BECAUSE THEY CAN CLIMB SO HARD??
wweeeennneee
PERFE EYE
EER REEM
10 kg
NO!! IT IS DEVELOPED ONLY BY USIN' LOTSA HOOKS, WEIGHTS & EXPENSIVE CREAMS!!
©Tknight

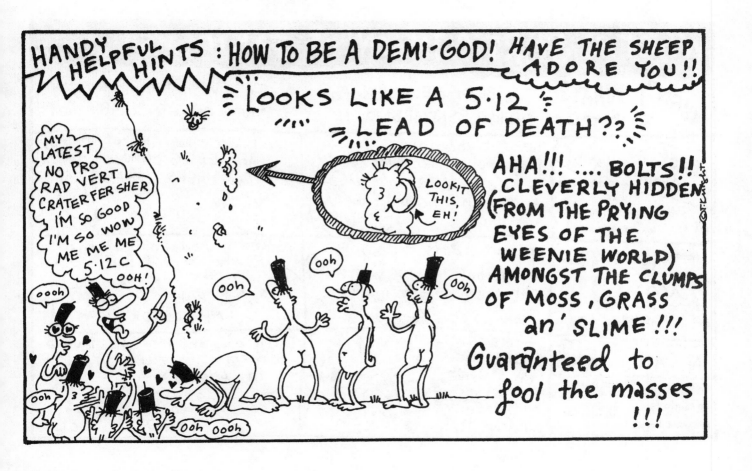

Where SPORT CLIMBIN' is takin' us....
WHEN?
WHAT?
The BEST METAPHOR fer Ethical SKWABBLIN'!!
The FURST THING they say to MUM after a CLIMBIN' TRIP!!
BACK IN DA GOODOL' DAYS!
Hemp rope
Hexes
Dinosaurs
E·B·S
pitons
woolly mammoths
THE dirt under yer fingernails haz come to life & iz talkin' to YOU in ANGLO SAXON!!
Iff I get a job AN' cut my hair AN' not go climbin' fer TWO WEEKS... WILLYA DO MY LAUNDRY?!
lycra
T·C·U·S
Flexie friends
NOW!
sliders
glasnost
Lynn Hill
Epileptic dogs rolling in a halibut carcass!
Wrrroof
SINCE I red-pointed that twelve-d that Dad AIDED in the sixties... WILLYA DO MY LAUNDRY?!
IN DA FUTURE!!
arthritis
cancer from steroids
no rainforests
acid rain wastelands
one piece lycra
SOMEONE CUTTING SHEET METAL WITH A CHAINSAW!
I fell off an' lost the tourna-ment all cuz of a STAIN on my LYCRA so.... WILLYA DO MY LAUNDRY??
©T.Knight

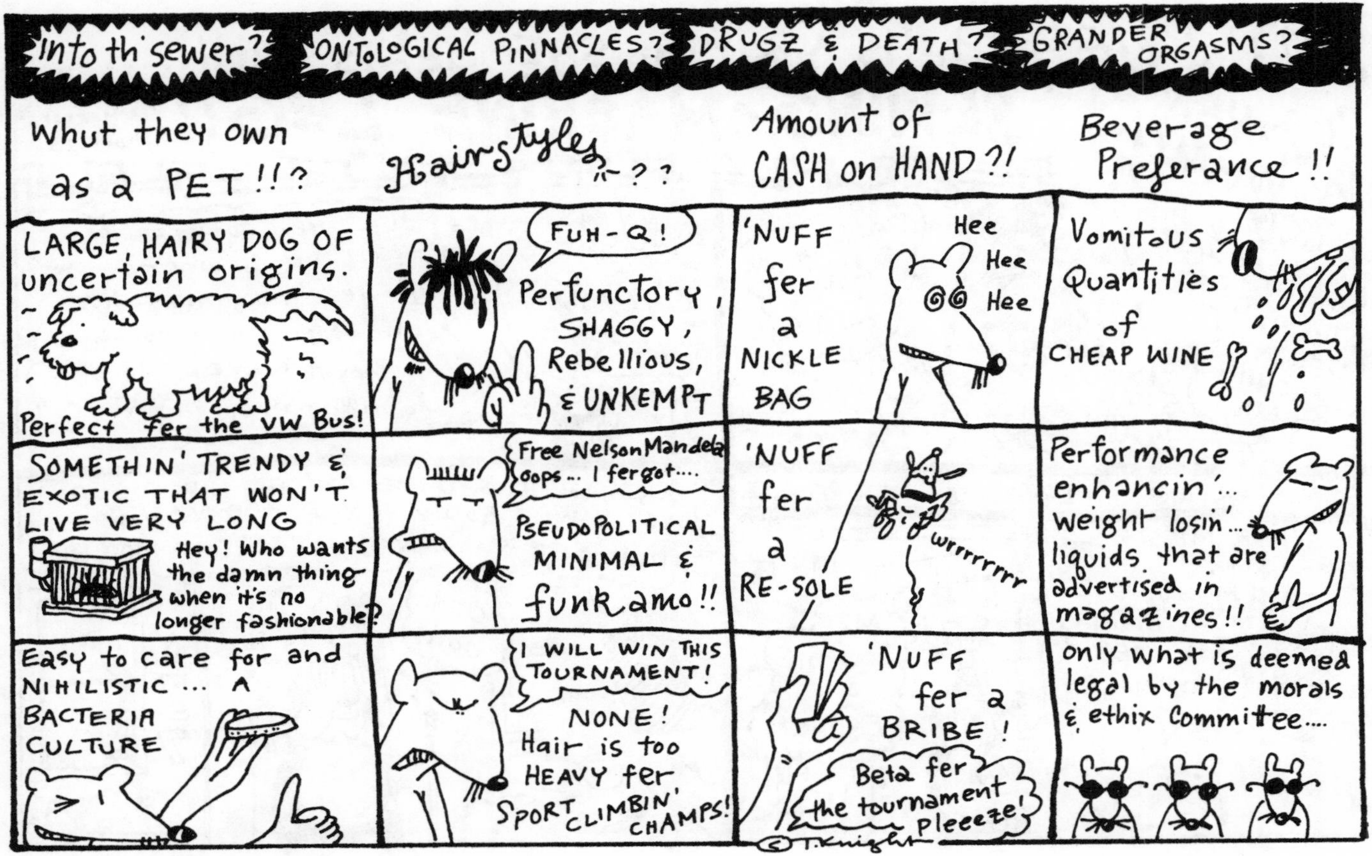
Into th' sewer?
ONTOLOGICAL PINNACLES?
DRUGZ & DEATH?
GRANDER ORGASMS?
Whut they own as a PET!!?
Hairstyles??
Amount of CASH on HAND?!
Beverage Preferance!!
LARGE, HAIRY DOG OF uncertain origins.
Perfect fer the VW Bus!
FUH-Q!
Perfunctory, SHAGGY, Rebellious, & UNKEMPT
'NUFF fer a NICKLE BAG
Hee Hee Hee
Vomitous Quantities of CHEAP WINE
SOMETHIN' TRENDY & EXOTIC THAT WON'T LIVE VERY LONG
Hey! Who wants the damn thing when it's no longer fashionable?
Free Nelson Mandela oops... I fergot....
PSEUDOPOLITICAL MINIMAL & funkamo!!
'NUFF fer a RE-SOLE
wrrrrrrr
Performance enhancin'... weight losin'... liquids that are advertised in magazines!!
Easy to care for and NIHILISTIC... A BACTERIA CULTURE
I WILL WIN THIS TOURNAMENT!
NONE! Hair is too HEAVY fer SPORT CLIMBIN' CHAMPS!
'NUFF fer a BRIBE!
Beta fer the tournament Pleeeze!
only what is deemed legal by the morals & ethix Committee....
© T. Knight

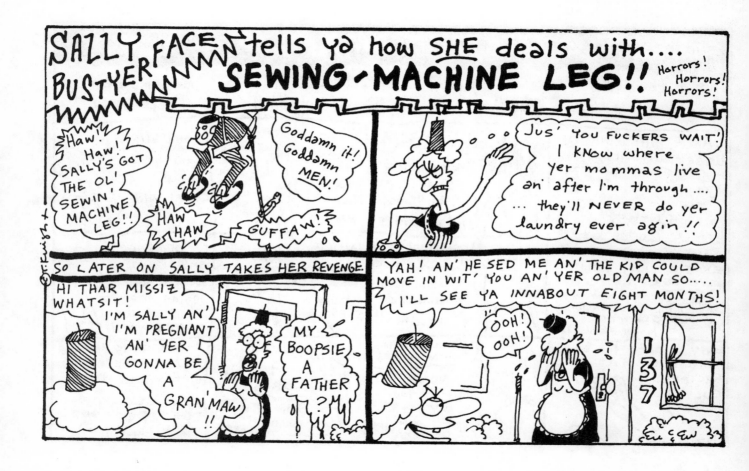

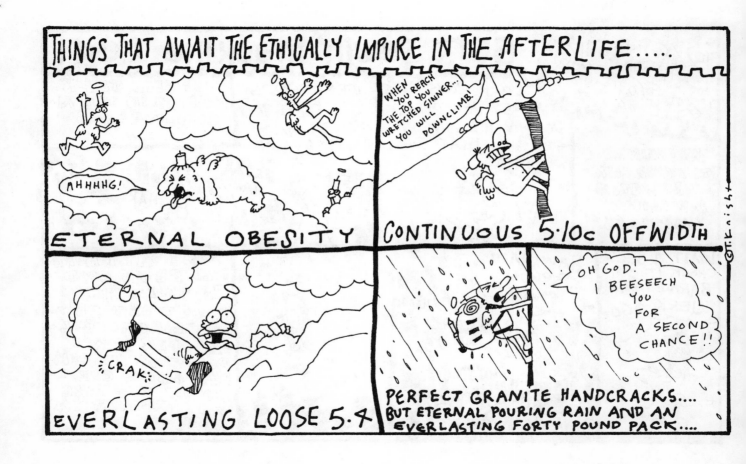

ROGER AN' SOME PALS HAVE STOPPED FER A REST ON THE GLACIER! CAN U SPOT 3 ERRORS THEY HAVE MADE??
ROGER! ROGER! HELP! HELP! I FELL INNA SLOT! GET ME OUT!!
ROGER! THERZ A FROZEN FLUFFY MAMMOTH DOWN HERE!
ANSWERZ ① ROGER'S Baloney sandwich has MAYO on it which doesn't keep well in the hot sun. ② ROGER'S BEER IS IN HIS PACK; It should be cooling in the snow. ③ "WOOLLY" Mammoth! NOT "FLUFFY". Jeez!!

A FIELD GUIDE TO MODERN DAY NORTH AMERICAN....
WINTER CLIMBERS!

	assorted characteristix	what they will be REINCARNATED as!	whut to get them fer CHRISTMAS	Field-guide KWIK-CHEK!
I LIKE IT! backcountry SKIER	• snot blob on *lip* • tells lies • devious tendancies	a refridgerator	mask, fins & a SNORKLE	(shown here breaking trail)
I LUV IT! winter MOUNTAINEER	• small watery eyes • cute but dull • picks nose • hairy (females particularily)	a species of mould that grows on peanut butter remains inside of a JERRY-TUBE!	set of matching tie and handkerchief.	spewing odious oaths
it GIVES MEE A BONER! ice CLIMBER	• eyes fail to focus • speaks french • luminous (!) hemmerhoids • severe nervous tic	Game Show Host	box of condoms, plus "Safesex" manual plus reading lessons	woo woo woo (approach with CAUTION!)

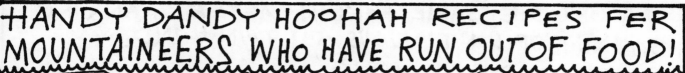

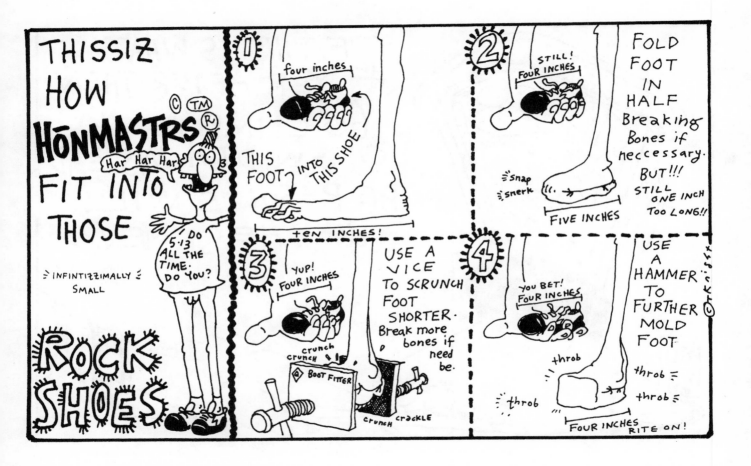

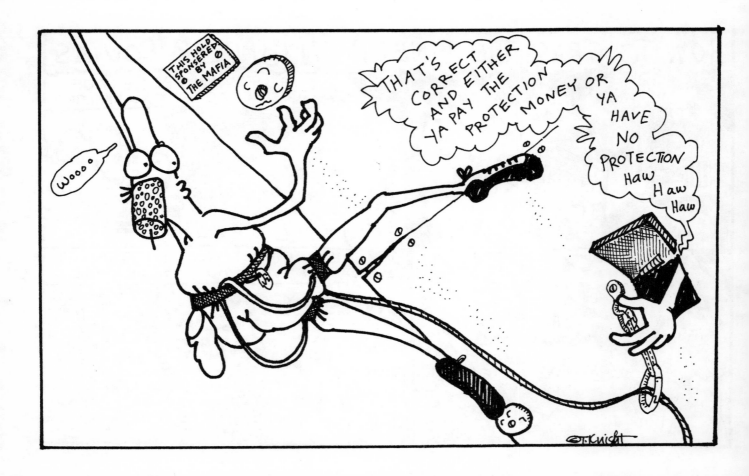

AN ANIMAL RIGHTS ACTIVIST HAS STOLEN A WHOLE BUNCH OF AVALANCHE POODLES. HE ABHORS THIS BRUTAL USE OF THESE CUTE AND FLUFFY LITTLE VER-SIONS OF MAN'S BEST FRIEND. HE WILL GRANT THESE POODLES THEIR FREEDOM.....

IT'S JUST DISGUSTING THAT SOMEONE WOULD WILLFULLY SENT AN INNOCENT POODLE TO IT'S DOOM....

HE WILL RELEASE THE POOD-LES IN THE PRISTINE BEAUTY OF THE SNOW CLAD MOUNT-AINS.

BE FREE LITTLE DOGGIES!!

THE POODLES HAVE BEEN TRAINED TO SEEK OUT AND TEST SLOPES WITH POTEN-TIAL AVALANCHE HAZARD.

IT IS A WRETCHED INEVITA--BILITY.

A PUZZIL PLEEZER! IDENTIFY THE CLIMBER MOST LIKELY TO PLACE A BOLT !!!

① YOSEMITE EX-HARDMAN recently released from prison. Has never free climbed.

② HOT EURO-CHICK metabolically enhanced sport climbin champ.

③ MIDDLE AGED ACCOUNTANT whose wife just left him for another woman.

T. O Knight

Now.... IDENTIFY THE CLIMBER MOST LIKELY TO WHINE ABOUT A BOLT!!

①

FOSSILIZED GUIDEBOOK WRITER and member-of-the-board-of-directors who hasn't climbed harder then 5.6 since 1975

②

TORMENTED SOLO CLIMBER with deep seated superstitions and recurring dreams about tomatoes.

③

LUNATIC ICE CLIMBER with few or no functioning brain cells.

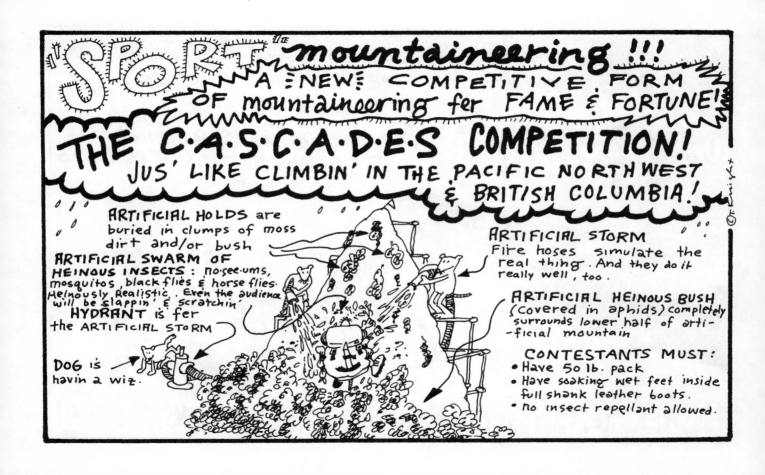

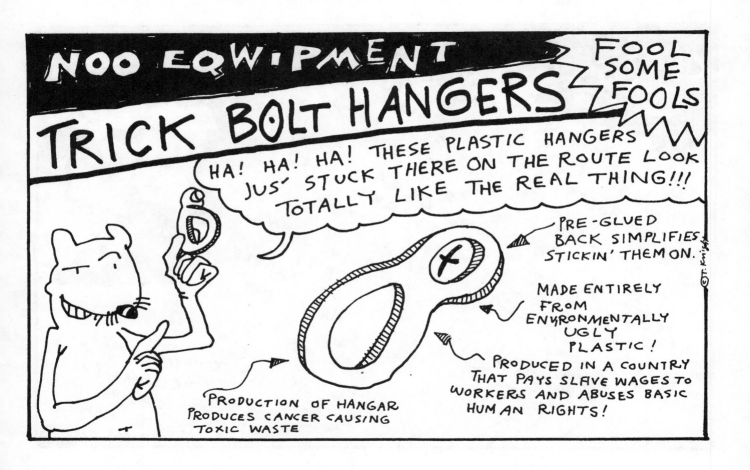

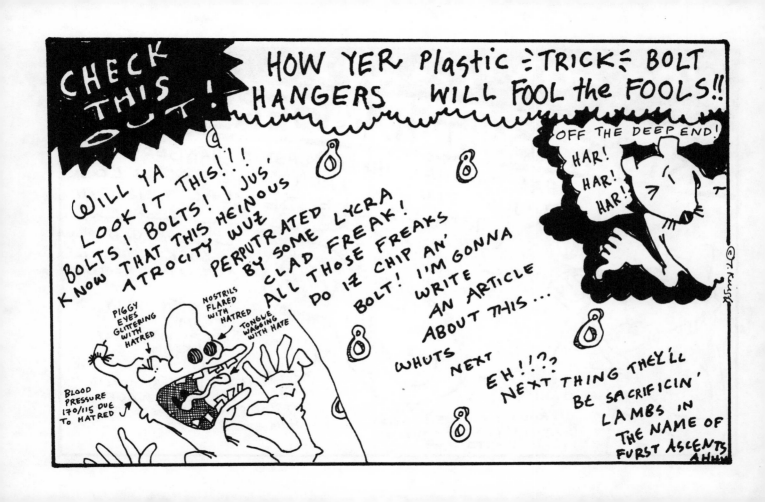

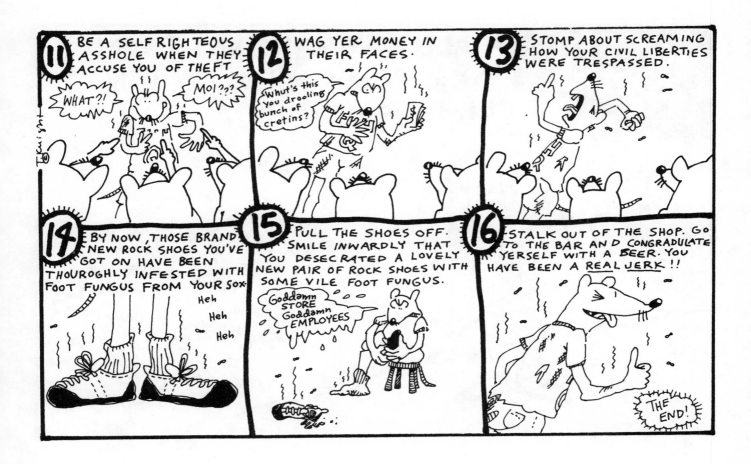

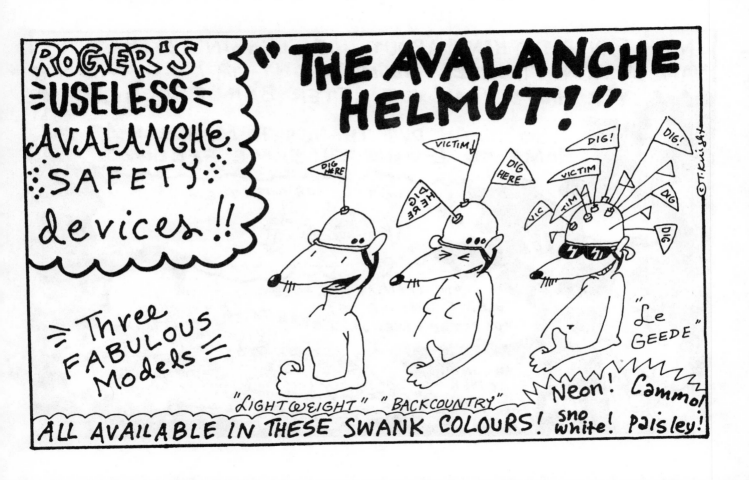

ROGER'S HEINOUS DREAM ≡ of the ≡ MORALS AND ETHICS NASTIES

"IT was after a crappy day of climbin'....
I'd tried that 5·11b pumping rattly-finger crack
I'd HUNG!
I couldn't SLEEP."

"I WUZ LYIN' THERE WIDE AWAKE WHEN THERE WAS A CLINK CLINK AT MY WINDOW.
I FELT THE FEAR LIKE A HOT IRON POKER."

MY THROAT TIGHTENED AROUND A SCREAM!

♪We hear♪ YOU HUNG on a 5·11 today♪

AAAAAA AAAAAA

T. Knight

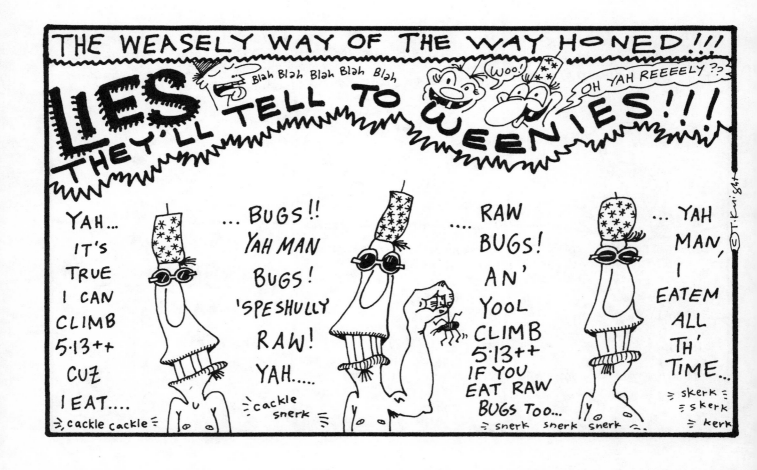

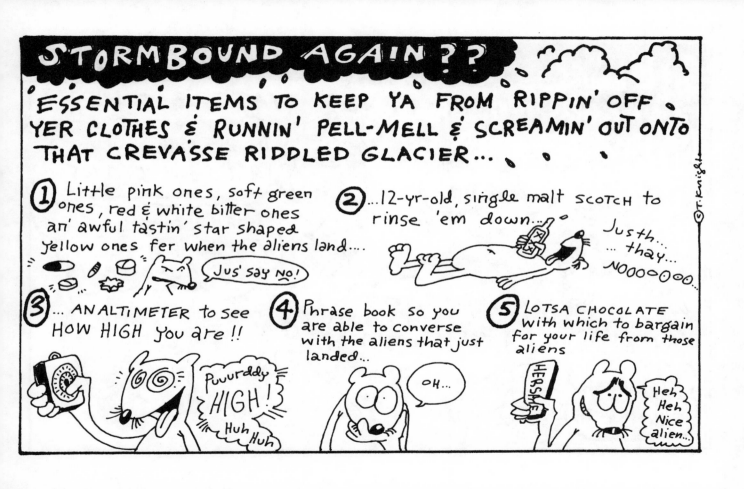

STORM BOUND MEDITATIONS...

WHAT TO DO ON YER FOURTH STRAIGHT DAY OF BEIN' STUCK IN THAT SNOWCAVE WITH THREE OTHER TOTAL JERKS.

① TRY to WIGGLE each of yer Toes individually.

> Damn
> ...all but the second smallest.

② COUNT the HAIRS on yer FOREARM.

> four thousand and two hundred thirty six
> four thousand and two hundred thirty seven
> four thousand and two hundred thirty eight
> four thousand and two hundred thirty NINE

③ ORGANIZE yer telekinetic POWERS & EVOLVE the spider hangin up thar.

ommm   WHEEE

④ USE those same telekinetic powers to make yer tentmates <u>HATE</u> chocklit!!

> OOOH YUCK
> BARF-O
> HERE! HAVE IT ALL
> YuuuuuuucK!!!

© T. Knight

File Yer STYLE !! BE HONED to the BONE !!

FAB   MINT   HEY

RAD   WOW

TAKE THIS KWIK TEST IN ORDER TO KEEP A BREAST OF THE LATEST !!!

① COMPLETE the SEQUENCE : 5.13c , 5.13d , 5.9 offwidth , 5.14 ????

② How many pounds of flesh have been left in cracks at Joshua Tree ??   YUUUCK

③ WRITE A LETTER TO A CLIMBIN' MAG ON HOW MANY FINGERS ROGER'S HOLDIN' UP AN WHY ?

Roger →

④ Why should lycra be made disposable ??

⑤ WHICH OF THE FOLLOWING HAS THE SMALLEST BRAIN ?
  • A HALIBUT ?
  • GOO IN THE BATH DRAIN ?
  • PLASTIC POP BOTTLE ?
  • SOMEONE WHO CHOPS OTHER PEOPLE'S CLIMBS ?
  • A MANHOLE COVER ?
  • SOMEONE WHO SLAMS IN BOLTS ?

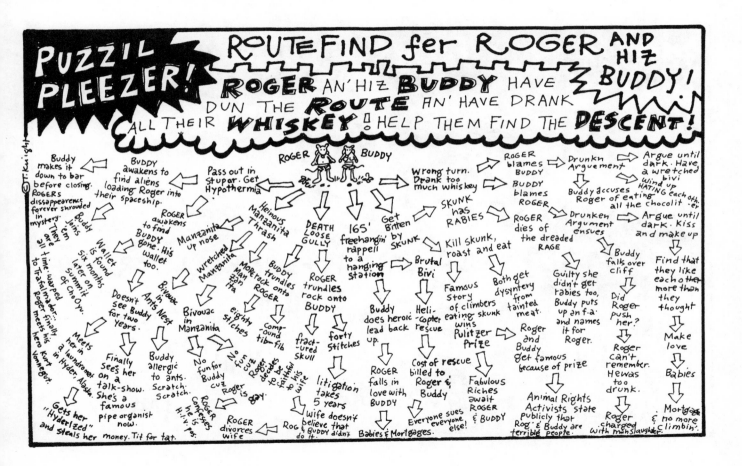

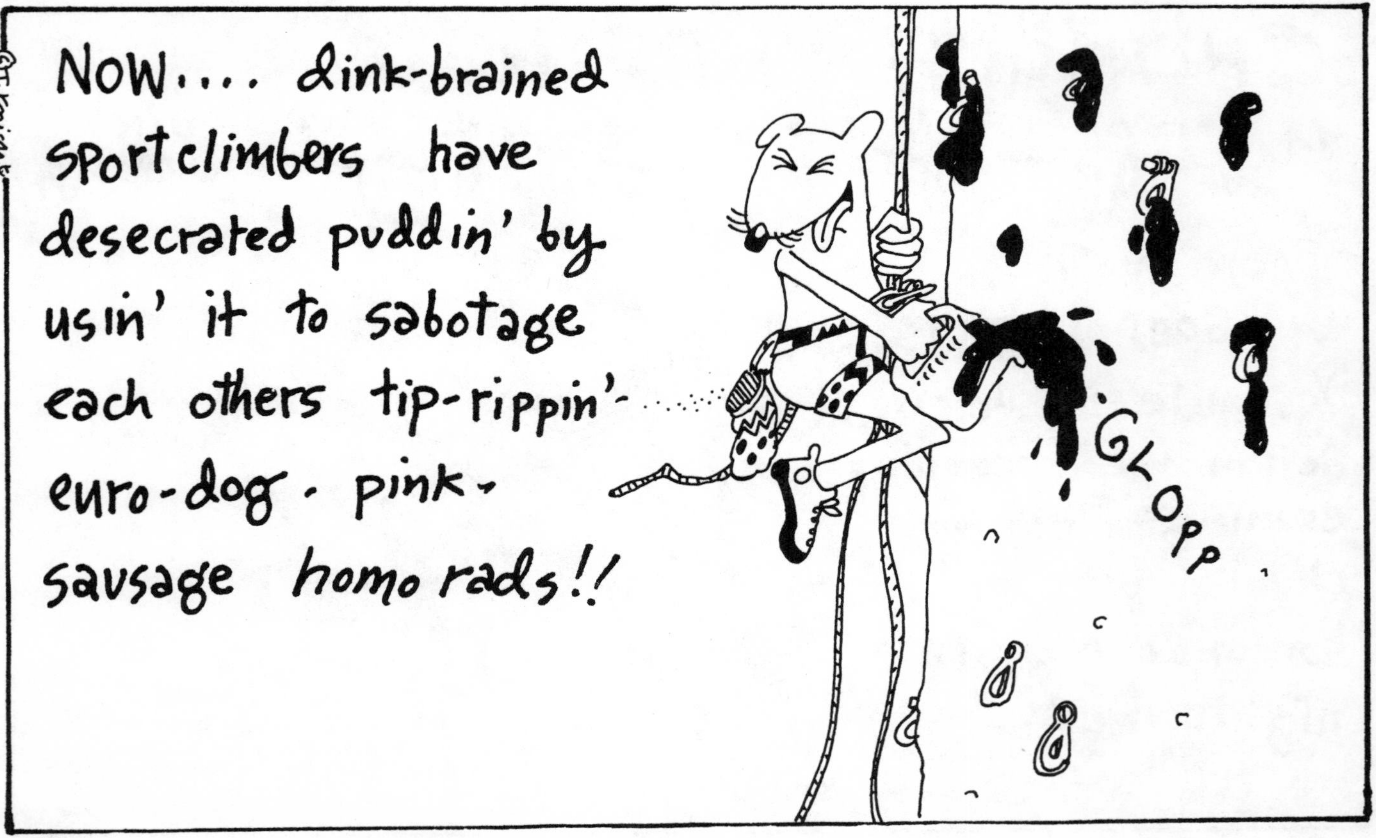
©T. Knight
NOW.... dink-brained sportclimbers have desecrated puddin' by usin' it to sabotage each others tip-rippin'-euro-dog-pink-sausage homo rads!!
GLOPP

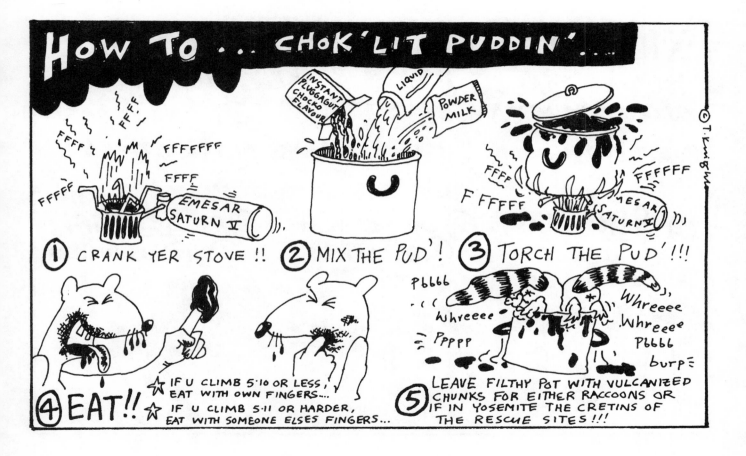

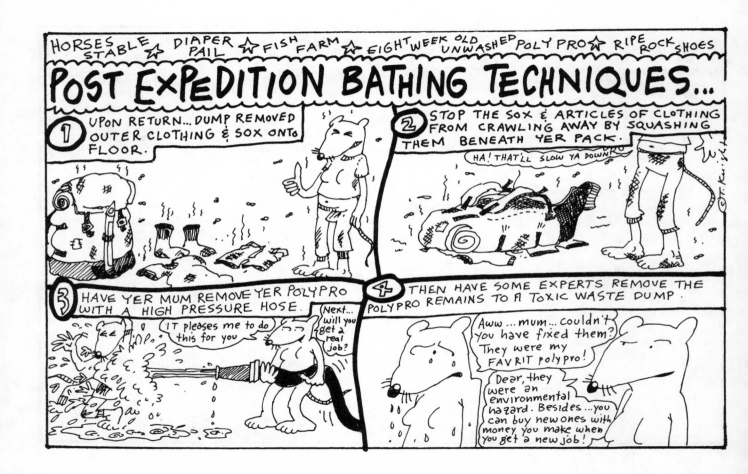

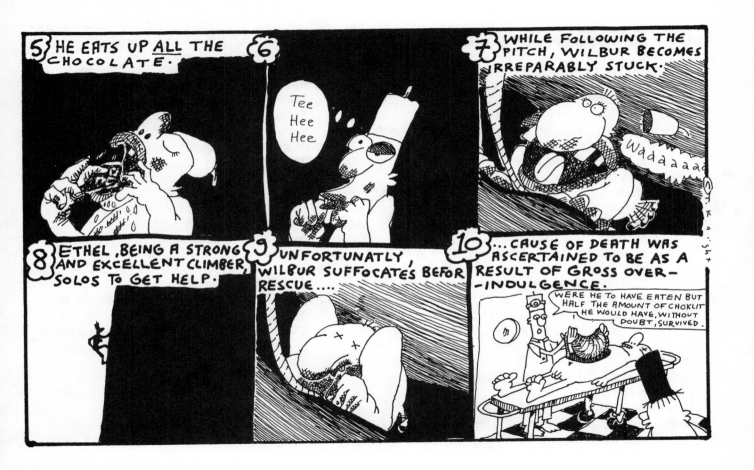

Menasha Ridge Press Books

Dirk Davidson

Beyond Sportdiving: Deepwater Adventures on the Shipwrecks of the Atlantic Coast, Brad Sheard

Diver's Guide to Underwater America, Kate Kelley and John Shobe

Shipwrecks: Diving the Graveyard of the Atlantic, Roderick M. Farb

Shipwrecks of Southern California, Bonnie J. Cardone and Patrick Smith

Boatbuilder's Manual, Charles Walbridge, editor

Smoky Mountains Trout Fishing Guide, Don Kirk

Fishing the Great Lakes of the South: An Angler's Guide to the TVA System, Don and Joann Kirk

A Fishing Guide to Kentucky's Major Lakes, Arthur B. Lander, Jr.

A Canoeing and Kayaking Guide to the Streams of Florida, Volume I, North Central Peninsula and Panhandle, Elizabeth F. Carter and John L. Pearce

A Canoeing and Kayaking Guide to the Streams of Florida, Volume II Central and South Peninsula, Lou Glaros and Doug Sphar

Appalachian Whitewater, Volume I, The Southern Mountains, Bob Sehlinger, Don Otey, Bob Benner, William Nealy, and Bob Lantz

Appalachian Whitewater, Volume II, The Central Mountains, Ed Grove, Bill Kirby, Charles Walbridge, Ward Eister, Paul Davidson, and Dirk Davidson

Appalachian Whitewater, Volume III, The Northern Mountains, John Connelly and John Porterfield

Northern Georgia Canoeing, Bob Sehlinger and Don Otey

Southern Georgia Canoeing, Bob Sehlinger and Don Otey

A Canoeing and Kayaking Guide to the Streams of Kentucky, Bob Sehlinger

A Canoeing and Kayaking Guide to the Streams of Ohio, Volume I, Richard Combs and Stephen E. Gillen

A Canoeing and Kayaking Guide to the Streams of Ohio, Volume II, Richard Combs and Stephen E. Gillen

A Canoeing and Kayaking Guide to the Streams of Tennessee, Volume I, Bob Sehlinger and Bob Lantz

A Canoeing and Kayaking Guide to the Streams of Tennessee, Volume II, Bob Sehlinger and Bob Lantz

Modern Outdoor Survival, Dwight R. Schuh
Emergency Medical Procedures for the Outdoors,
    Patient Care Publications, Inc.

Guide and Map to the Uwharrie Trail, G. Nicholas
    Hancock
Harsh Weather Camping, Sam Curtis